REVISION BOOK

Grade 4 Music Theory

to be used in conjunction with **All-In-One to Grade 5**

Comprehensive to the requirements of both ABRSM and Trinity Guildhall syllabuses

By Rachel Billings

Published by Aaron publications
www.aaronpublications.co.uk

© Rachel Billings
All rights reserved

Reproducing any part of this book in any form is illegal and forbidden by the Copyright Designs and Patent Act 1988

Printed in Great Britain by Pelican Trust Ltd. Lincoln.

© Unauthorized photocopying is illegal

Preface

This revision booklet accompanies 'All-In-One to Grade 5' and provides practice for topics covered in Associated Board (ABRSM) and Trinity Guildhall Grade 4 music theory exams. Many questions (especially those in the General Exercise section) test a pupil's comprehension of more than one topic at once and wording, wherever possible, is the same as that used by the relevant exam board so that students will feel well prepared and confident in the final stages before an exam.

Rachel Billings BMus, GRNCM, PgDip.

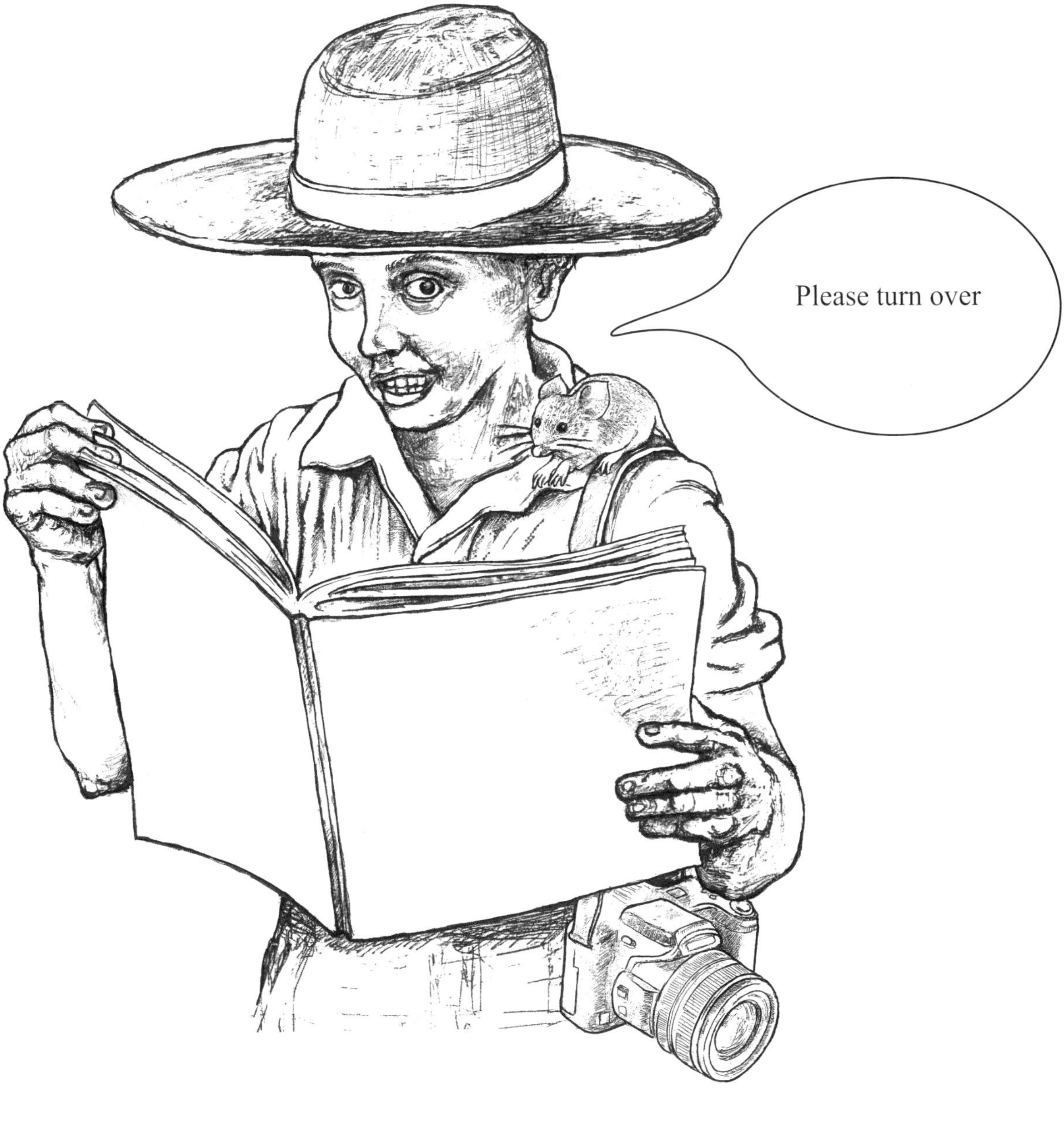
Please turn over

CONTENTS

Topics should be completed by all students except for the last chapter which need be completed by Trinity Guildhall students only.

CHAPTER	GRADE 4 TOPICS	PAGE
1. NOTATION	**ALTO CLEF** • Notation and Transposition of Octave	2
2. TIME	**SIMPLE AND COMPOUND TIME** • Time Signatures, Beaming Tails, Grouping of Rests and Tied Notes • Irregular divisions: Duplets • Conversion of Simple Time to Compound Time, and Vice Versa **NOTE AND REST VALUES** • Breves, Double Dots	6 9 10 11
3. TONALITY	**MAJOR AND MINOR KEYS** • Keys and Technical Note Names • Accidentals: Double Sharps, Double Flats and Enharmonic Equivalents • Primary Chords : Tonic, Subdominant and Dominant **THE CHROMATIC SCALE** **CHROMATIC INTERVALS**	14 16 17 18 19
GENERAL EXERCISES	Questions may be upon *any* of the above topics plus the following: *Foreign Words, General Signs, Ornaments, Orchestral Instruments, Words and Rhythms*	22

TRINITY GUILDHALL EXAMS ONLY (Topics in this section are beyond ABRSM Grade 4 requirements)	PAGE
Broken Chords, Writing 4-part Primary Chords For SATB (root position), Labeling Chord Inversions, Dominant 7th Chords, Adding a Bass Line to a Tune Or Vice Versa, Cadences , Orchestral Instruments	29

© Unauthorized photocopying is illegal

CHAPTER ONE
NOTATION

CHAPTER ONE, NOTATION, Alto Clef

ALTO CLEF
Notation and Transposition Of Octave

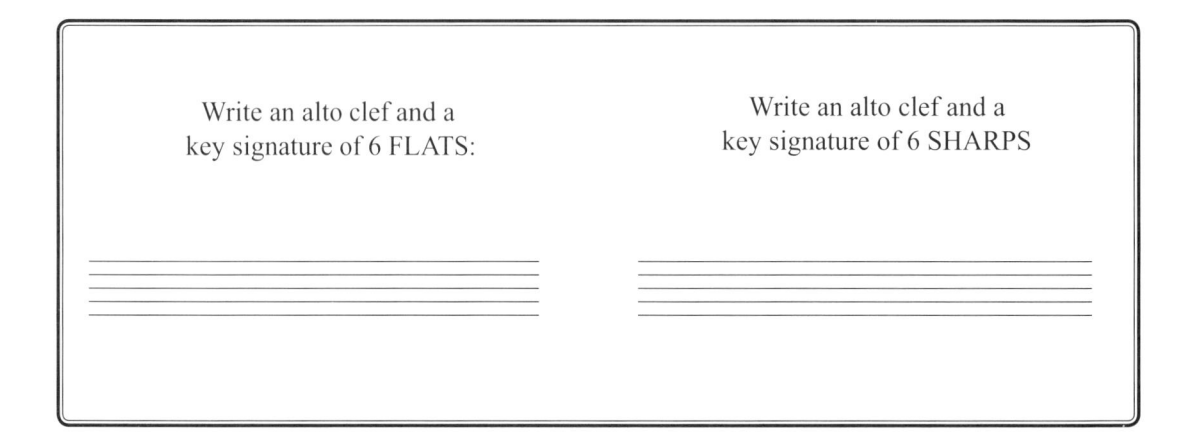

Write an alto clef and a key signature of 6 FLATS:

Write an alto clef and a key signature of 6 SHARPS

---

1. Rewrite the following passage at the same pitch using the alto clef.

Mahler, Symphony No.9 (1st mvt)

a)

Mozart, Symphony in G minor, K550

b)

2. Rewrite the following passages one octave lower in the alto clef.

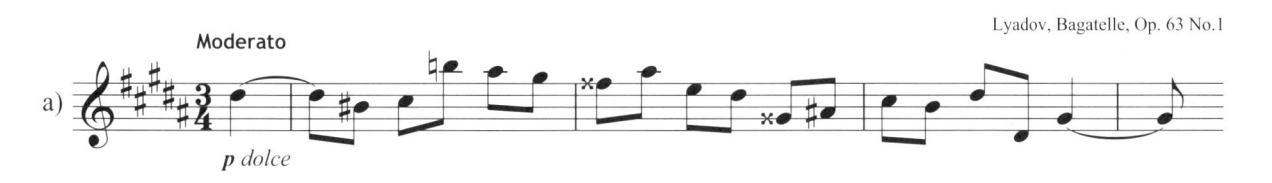

a) Moderato — Lyadov, Bagatelle, Op. 63 No.1

p dolce

b) Allegro assai — Beethoven, Piano Sonata, Op. 57 'Appassionata' (1st mvt)

cresc. *f* *p*

CHAPTER ONE, NOTATION, Alto Clef

3. Rewrite the following passages one octave higher in the alto clef.

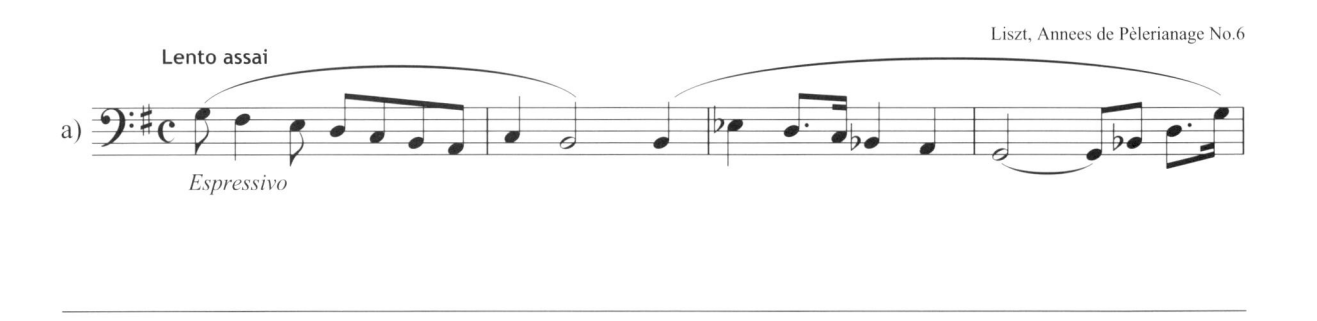

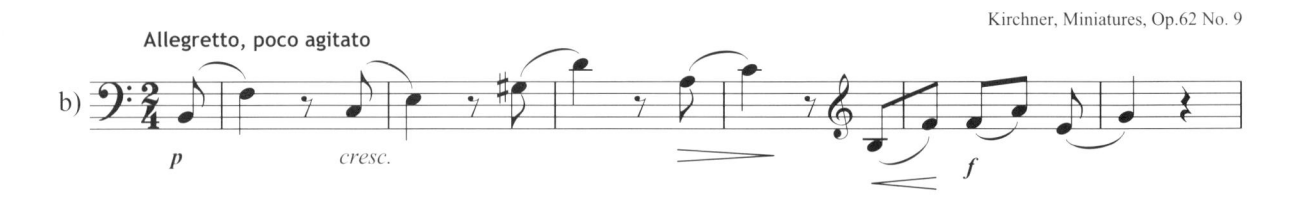

Liszt, Annees de Pèlerianage No.6

a) **Lento assai**

Espressivo

Kirchner, Miniatures, Op.62 No. 9

b) **Allegretto, poco agitato**

p   *cresc.*   *f*

© *Unauthorized photocopying is illegal*

CHAPTER TWO
TIME

CHAPTER TWO, TIME, Simple and Compound Time

SIMPLE TIME & COMPOUND TIME

Time Signatures, Beaming Tails, Grouping of Rests and Tied Notes

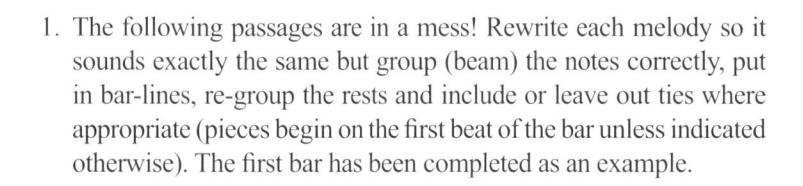

1. The following passages are in a mess! Rewrite each melody so it sounds exactly the same but group (beam) the notes correctly, put in bar-lines, re-group the rests and include or leave out ties where appropriate (pieces begin on the first beat of the bar unless indicated otherwise). The first bar has been completed as an example.

2. Describe the time signatures as simple or compound, duple, triple or quadruple.

J.S.Bach, Partita No. 4 (Gigue)

a)

Time signature .... (simple or compound, duple, triple or quadruple)

Schumann, 'Song of Spring', from Album for the Young

b)

Time signature .... (simple or compound, duple, triple or quadruple)

© Unauthorized photocopying is illegal

Ravel, Piano Concerto (1st mvt)

c)

Time signature .... (simple or compound, duple, triple or quadruple)

J.S.Bach, 48 Preludes & Fugues, Bk II (Prelude No.4)

d)

Time signature .... (simple or compound, duple, triple or quadruple)

Hindemith, Trio No. 2 (1st mvt)

e)

Time signature .... (simple or compound, duple, triple or quadruple)

CHAPTER TWO, TIME, Simple and Compound Time

Brahms, Piano concerto No. 1

f)

Time signature .... (simple or compound, duple, triple or quadruple)

Grieg, Op. 57 No.6 ('Home-sickness')

g)

Time signature .... (simple or compound, duple, triple or quadruple)

Lalo, Concerto in D minor (1st mvt)

h)

Time signature .... (simple or compound, duple, triple or quadruple)

Irregular Divisions: Duplets

1. Put the time signatures before each of the following tunes.

2. Add the missing bar-lines to the following extracts.

CHAPTER TWO, TIME, Simple and Compound Time

Conversion of Simple Time to Compound Time, and Vice Versa

Rewrite the following passages using the given time signatures. The effect should remain the same (the first bar has been completed as an example).

COMPOUND TO SIMPLE TIME

Chopin, Nocturne, Op.9 No.1

Kuhlau, Sonatina, Op.88 No.3 (2nd mvt)

SIMPLE TO COMPOUND TIME

Beethoven, Symphony No.9 (4th mvt)

Haydn, Symphony in F♯ minor (5th mvt)

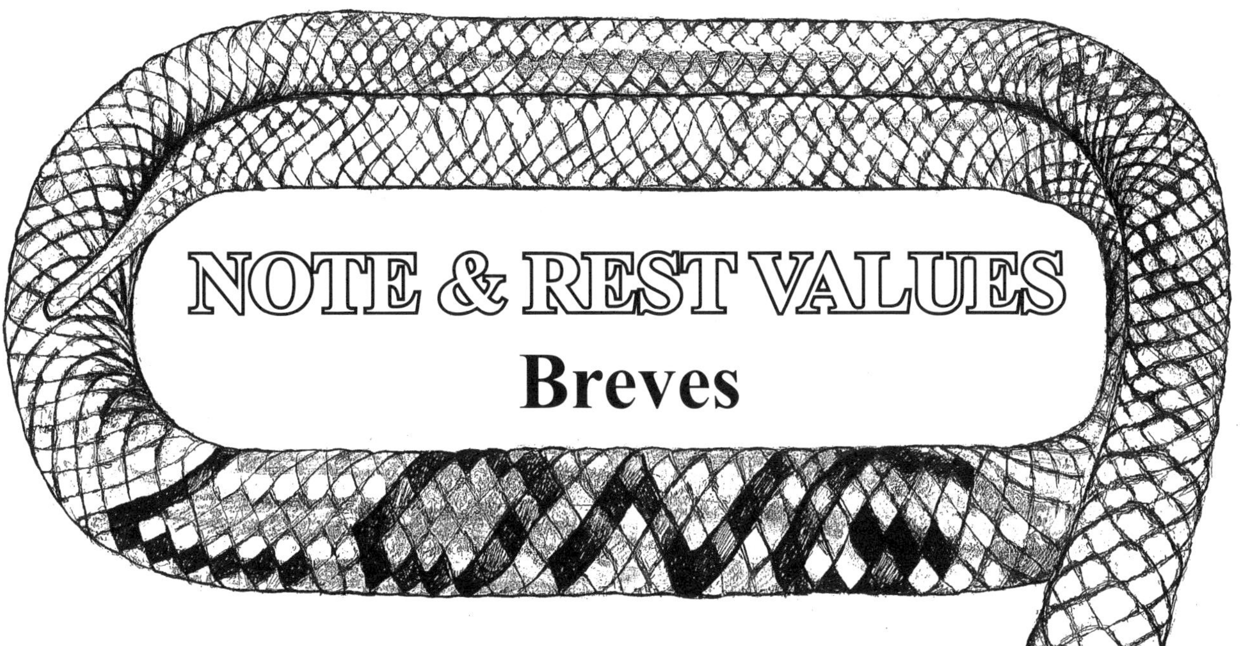

NOTE & REST VALUES
Breves

1. Rewrite these passages in notes and rests of *twice* the value and add the new time signatures required. The first bar has been completed as an example.

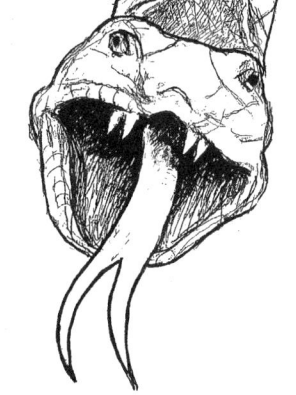

2. Rewrite these passages in notes and rests of *half* the value and add the new time signatures required.

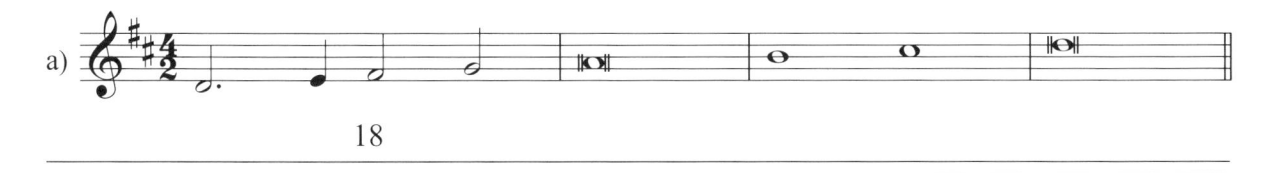

CHAPTER ONE, TIME, Note and Rest Values

Double Dots

1. Complete the following with the correct number:

   o ·· is worth .... crotchets
   .... quavers

   ♩ ·· is worth .... semiquavers
   .... demisemiquavers

   ♩ ·· is worth .... quavers
   .... semiquavers

   ♪ ·· is worth .... demisemiquavers

2. Add the missing bar-lines to these three melodies, which all begin on the first beat of the bar.

   Mozart, Fantasia in D minor

   a)

   Mozart, Piano concerto in C

   b)

   Haydn, Quartet in E

   c)

3. Rewrite these passages in notes and rests of *half* the value and add the new time signatures required.

   a)

   b)

CHAPTER THREE
TONALITY

CHAPTER THREE, TONALITY, Major and Minor Keys

MAJOR & MINOR KEYS

Keys and Technical Note Names

1. Name the key of each of the following melodies then write the technical names under each note marked with a number (watch out for whether the key is major or minor!).

Haydn, Keyboard Sonata, Hob. XVI No.49

a)

Key: _____ 1. _____ 2. _____ 3. _____
                     4. _____ 5. _____ 6. _____

J.S. Bach, 48 Preludes & Fugues, Bk.1 (Prelude No. 18)

b)

Key: _____ 1. _____ 2. _____ 3. _____
                     4. _____ 5. _____ 6. _____

Mendelssohn, Hebrides Overture

c)

Key: _____ 1. _____ 2. _____ 3. _____
                     4. _____ 5. _____ 6. _____

© Unauthorized photocopying is illegal

2 a) Write the "subdominant" of each of the keys named.

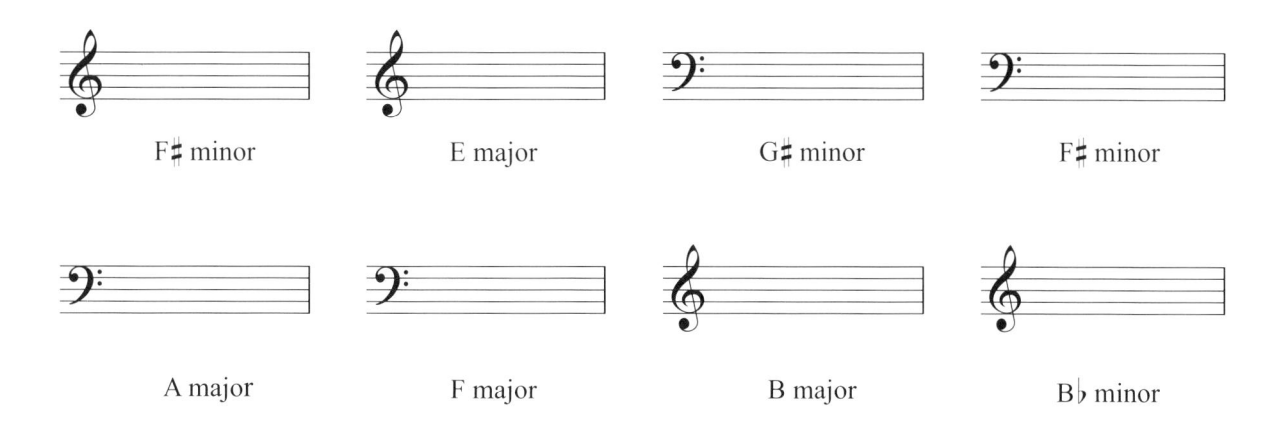

F# minor   E major   G# minor   F# minor

A major   F major   B major   Bb minor

b) Write the "mediant" of each of the keys named.

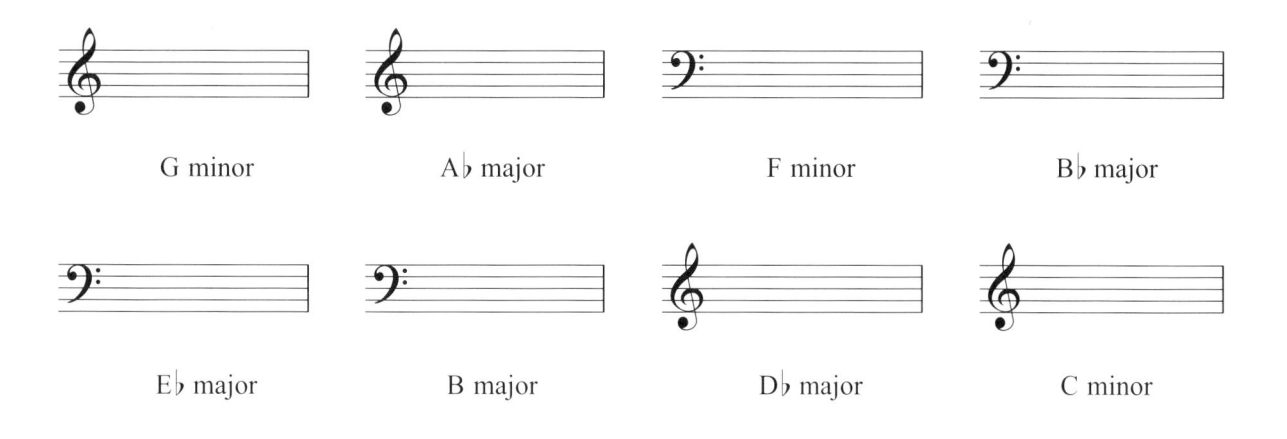

G minor   Ab major   F minor   Bb major

Eb major   B major   Db major   C minor

c) Write the "supertonic" of each of the keys named.

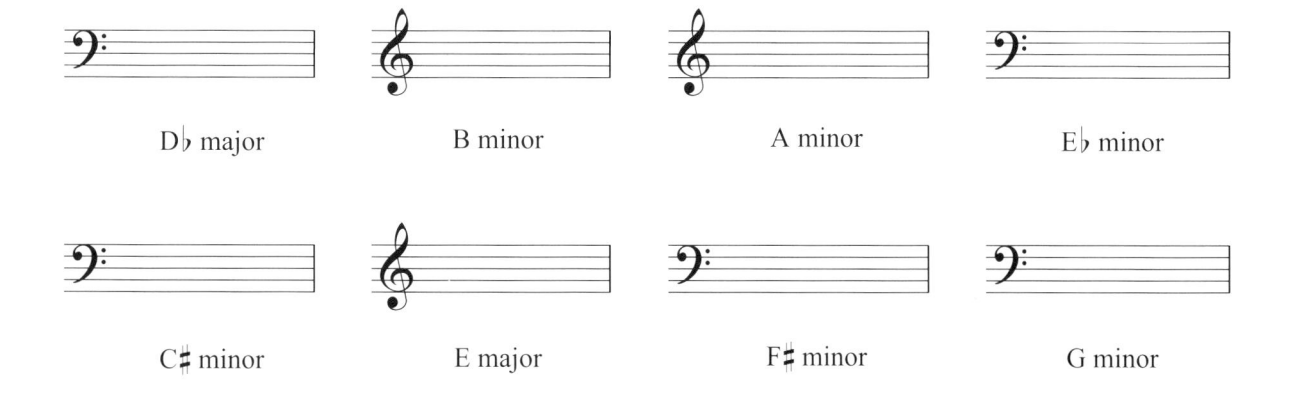

Db major   B minor   A minor   Eb minor

C# minor   E major   F# minor   G minor

CHAPTER THREE, TONALITY, Major and Minor Keys

Accidentals: Double sharps, Double flats and Enharmonic Equivalents

1. Write the **enharmonic equivalent** of the following scales using *sharps*, either with or without key signature (notice the clefs given).

Db major, ascending.
The enharmonic equivalent (using sharps) is .... which is written as follows:

Bb melodic minor, ascending and descending.
The enharmonic equivalent (using sharps) is .... which is written as follows:

2. Write the **enharmonic equivalent** of the following scales using *flats*, either with or without key signature (notice the clefs given).

B major, ascending.
The enharmonic equivalent (using flats) is .... which is written as follows:

G♯ melodic minor, ascending and descending.
The enharmonic equivalent (using flats) is .... which is written as follows:

Primary Chords:
Tonic, Subdominant, Dominant

Write the named triads as shown by the key signature (remember to include any accidentals if they are needed).

major key
subdominant chord

major key
tonic chord

minor key
subdominant chord

minor key
dominant chord

major key
dominant chord

minor key
dominant chord

major key
subdominant chord

major key
tonic chord

major key
subdominant chord

minor key
tonic chord

minor key
dominant chord

major key
tonic chord

major key
dominant chord

minor key
subdominant chord

CHAPTER THREE, TONALITY, The Chromatic Scale

THE CHROMATIC SCALE

1. Add the necessary accidentals to form chromatic scales. Watch out for the key signatures. Do not include unnecessary accidentals.

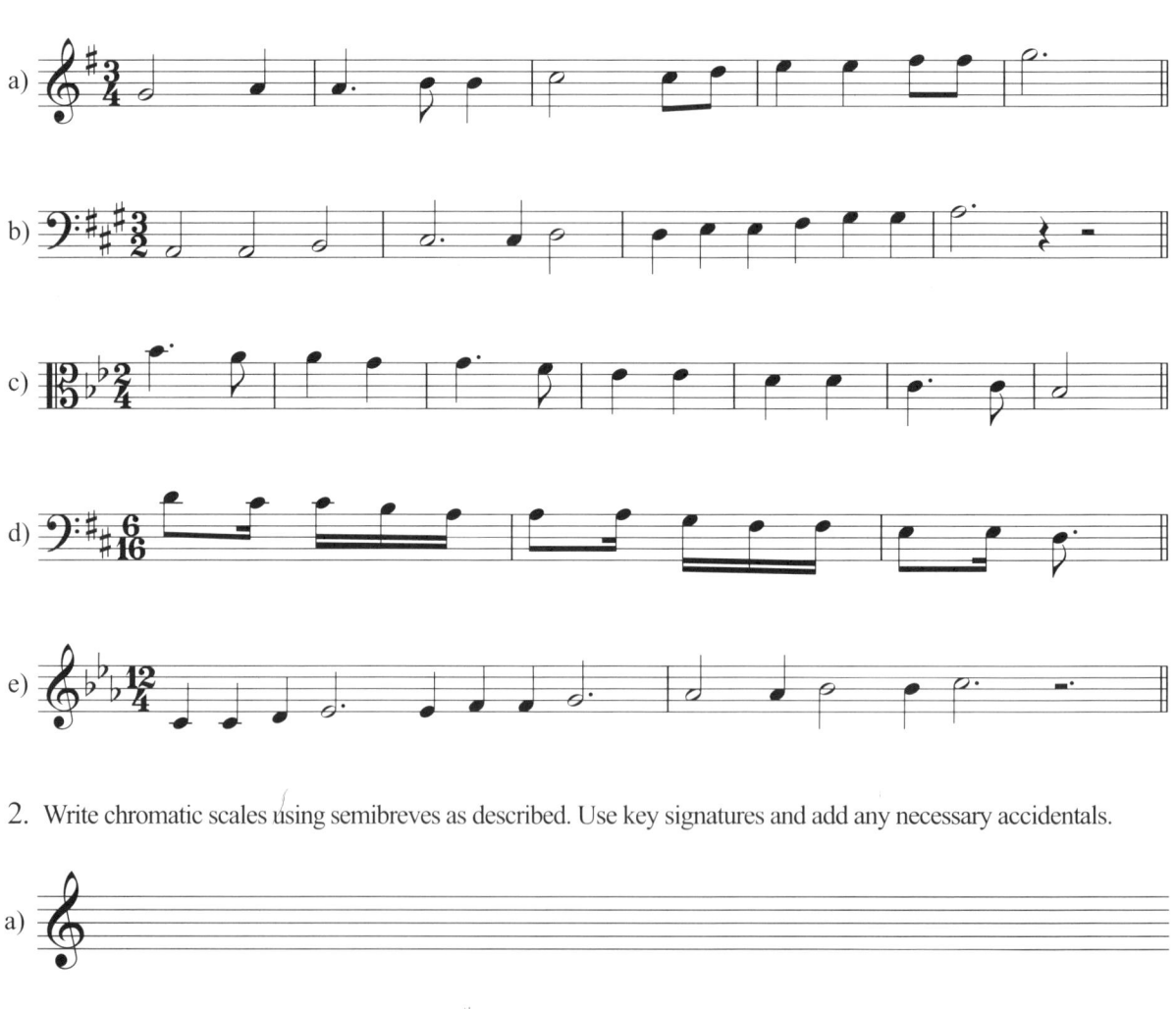

a)

b)

c)

d)

e)

2. Write chromatic scales using semibreves as described. Use key signatures and add any necessary accidentals.

a)

Ascending, starting on the mediant of F♯ minor.

b)

Descending, starting on the dominant of A♭ major.

c)

Ascending, starting on the submediant of F♯ minor.

CHROMATIC INTERVALS

1. Describe the difference between 'diatonic' and 'chromatic' intervals.

....

....

....

2. Give the full names (major 2nd, minor 3rd etc.) of the following intervals which may be either diatonic or chromatic. Identify the chromatic intervals by writing the letter Ⓒ next to the interval.

CHAPTER THREE, TONALITY, Chromatic Intervals

3. Describe fully each of the intervals (take note of the key signatures).

4. Give the full names of the following melodic intervals (e.g. major 3rd, minor 3rd etc.). Keep in mind the key signature and any accidentals which may have occurred earlier in the bar.

J.S.Bach, Toccata No. 5 in D major

a)

1. _____ 2. _____ 3. _____
4. _____ 5. _____ 6. _____

D. Shostakovich, Prelude No.24, Op.3

b)

1. _____ 2. _____ 3. _____
4. _____ 5. _____ 6. _____

© Unauthorized photocopying is illegal

Brahms, Piano Quintet Op.34 (1st mvt)

c)

1. _____ 2. _____ 3. _____
4. _____ 5. _____ 6. _____

Brahms, String Quartet, Op. 67 (2nd mvt)

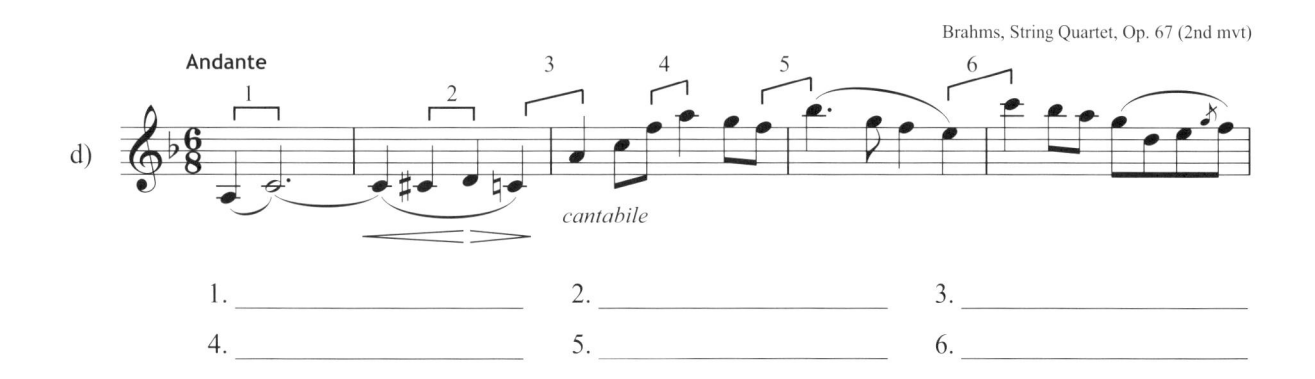

d) *cantabile*

1. _____ 2. _____ 3. _____
4. _____ 5. _____ 6. _____

Mozart, Piano concerto in A major, K.V. No. 488 (2nd mvt)

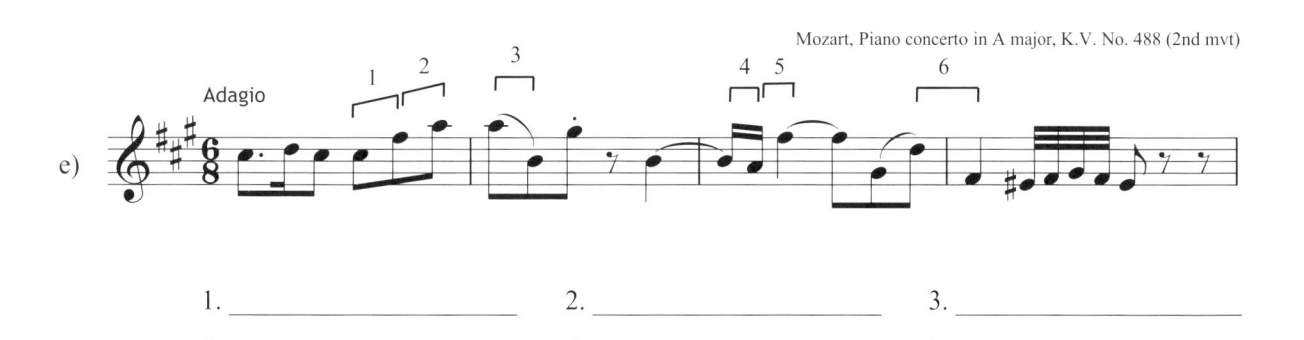

e) Adagio

1. _____ 2. _____ 3. _____
4. _____ 5. _____ 6. _____

J.S. Bach, Invention No.2

f)

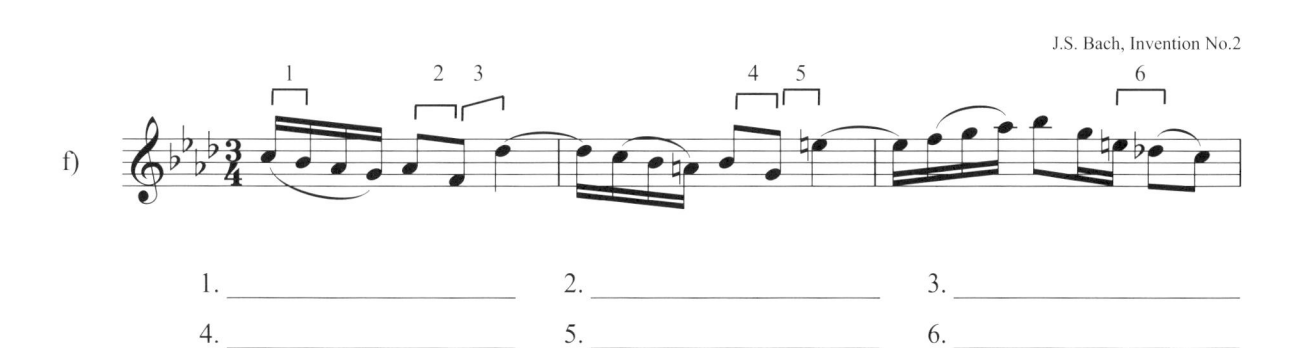

1. _____ 2. _____ 3. _____
4. _____ 5. _____ 6. _____

GENERAL EXERCISES

1. Write a rhythm on one note, with time signature and bar-lines to these words. Each syllable must be written under the note or notes to which it is to be sung.

Grandma read her many books whilst
Rocking in rhythm, back and forth.
Rickety old rocking chair,
Old and worn and worse for wear.

Rachel Billings

Rhythm _____

Words ....

Rhythm _____

Words ....

2. Below is an extract from J.S.Bach's French Suite No. III for Keyboard (Courante).

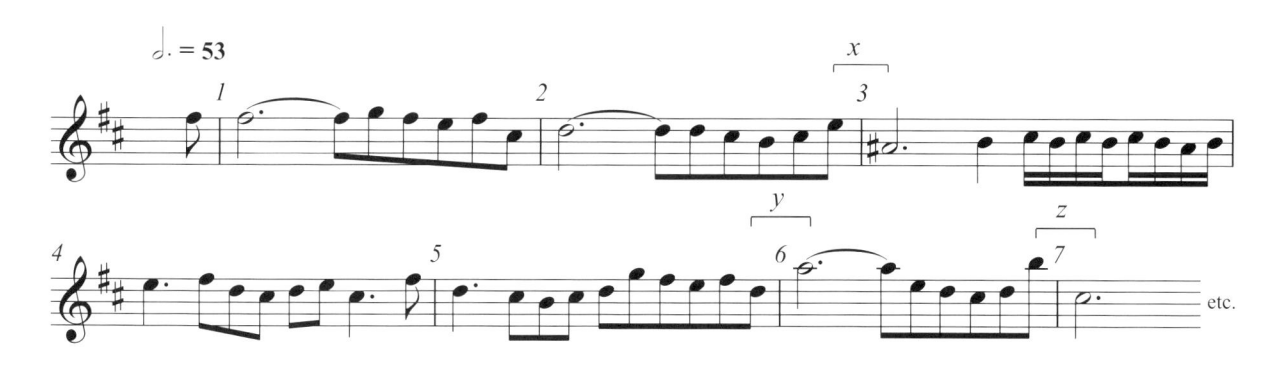

a) i) This piece begins in a minor key (bars 1- 4). Name the key ....

   ii) Which other key has the same key signature ? ....

b) i) Write the time signature at the beginning of the piece.

   ii) Circle two words which describe the time signature: *Simple*   *Compound*   *Duple*   *Triple*   *Quadruple*

   iii) Rewrite bar 3 in notes of *half* the value and add the time signature required.

c) Describe fully the intervals marked *x, y* and *z*

   x .... y .... z ....

d) Give the meaning of the following musical terms and circle one which best describes the speed of the given metronome marking (𝅗𝅥. = 53)

   Largo ma non troppo ....

   En dehors ....

   Morendo ....

   Pesante ....

   Allegro ....

   Tempo giusto ....

GENERAL EXERCISES

3. The following passage is from the first movement of Joseph Haydn's String Quartet Op.20, No.6. Look at it then answer the questions below.

a) i) Write the names of the instruments at the beginning of the piece.

   ii) How can the instrument on the top stave play two notes at the same time? Name the term used.

   ....

   ....

b) i) Explain the meaning of:

   Allegro di molto ....

   Scherzando ....

   'pizz.' ....

c) Name the ornament used in bar 2 ....

   bar 4 ....

d) Write the top part in bars 1-2 in notes and rests of *twice* the value and add the new time signature required.

e) i) Name the key ....

   ii) Which other key has the same key signature? ....

f) i) Identify the chords marked * as tonic, subdominant or dominant by writing their chord symbol beneath the stave.

   ii) Complete:

   These three chords are known as __ __ __ __ __ __ __ chords

g) i) Circle a mediant note on the top stave
   ii) Circle a dominant note on the bottom stave

h) Name the following clef then write the passage at the same pitch using the bass clef

.... clef

Bass clef

i) Compare bars 1-3 with bars 5-7. What do you notice?

....

....

....

GENERAL EXERCISES

4. The following is an extract from a duo sonata by Reinecke.

a) The top part is written for a non-transposing woodwind instrument which does not have a reed. Name both the instruments for which this sonata was written.

Instrument 1) ....

Instrument 2) ....

b) i) The key in bars 1-5 is B minor. Circle two bars next to each other which contain only notes from the dominant chord of this key.

   ii) Name the key from bar 6 onwards ....

   iii) Name the relative major/minor key of your answer to question 'bii', and write its scale on the stave below, with key signature.

   .... major/ minor (delete as appropriate)

c) Describe fully the intervals in brackets marked *u, v, w, x, y* and *z*.

   u .... v .... w ....

   x .... y .... z ....

d) Circle three neighbouring notes in the top part which ascend chromatically.

e) Rewrite bars 6-11 of the melody (the top stave) so that it sounds the same but using a time signature of $\frac{6}{8}$. Do *not* use a key signature but add the correct accidentals next to the notes.

GENERAL EXERCISES

f) Write one note which totals the same value as the following tied notes:

   𝅗𝅥. ⌣ ♪ = ...

g) Explain the meaning of:

   Allegro vivace ....

   Misterioso ....

   Più lento ....

   Quasi andante ....

   Ped. ✻ ....

h) i) Rewrite bar 6 of the top part using an ornament sign to replace the notes in brackets.

   ii) Name the ornament ....

i) In bars 1-5 (in B minor), find the following notes and identify them by writing the appropriate letter next to the note and circling the note.

   A. Supertonic note
   B. Mediant note
   C. Dominant note
   D. Leading note

© *Unauthorized photocopying is illegal*

TRINITY GUILDHALL EXAMS ONLY[1]

1. Write the following broken chords, using the correct key signature.

a) E♭ major tonic triad ascending in quavers. Use patterns of four notes each time and finish on the first E♭ above the stave.

b) A♭ major tonic triad descending in quavers. Use patterns of three notes each time and finish on middle C.

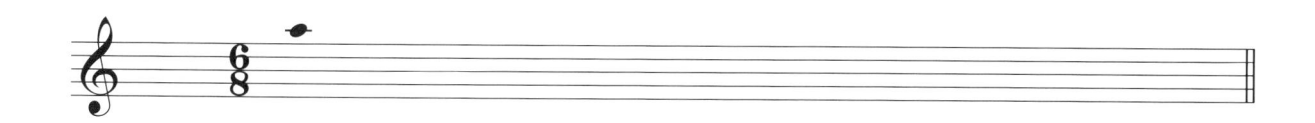

c) B♭ minor tonic triad ascending in minims. Use patterns of three notes each time and finish on the first F above the stave.

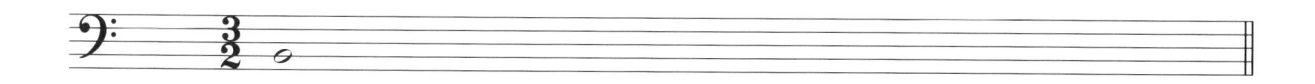

d) E minor tonic triad descending in semiquavers. Use patterns of four notes each time and finish on the E on the first line.

---

[1] Topics are for Trinity Guildhall students only. However the use of key signatures here (and throughout this booklet) corresponds to the ABRSM syllabus and in this respect exceeds Trinity Guildhall requirements.

2. Using crotchets, write out 4-part chords for SATB using the chords shown by the Roman numerals. Double the root in each case and make sure that each chord is in root position.

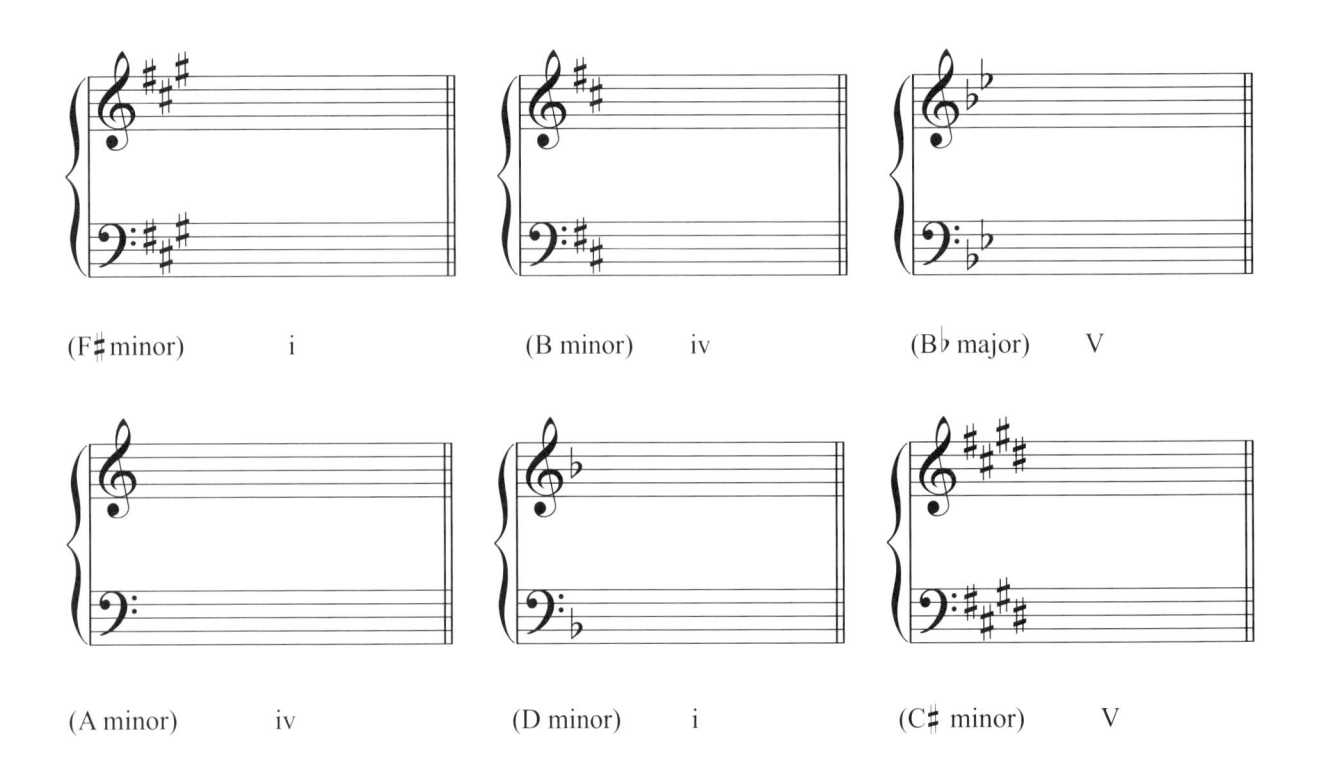

(F♯ minor)   i

(B minor)   iv

(B♭ major)   V

(A minor)   iv

(D minor)   i

(C♯ minor)   V

3. Label the chords and their inversions with Roman numerals below the stave and jazz chord symbols above to show the chord progression.

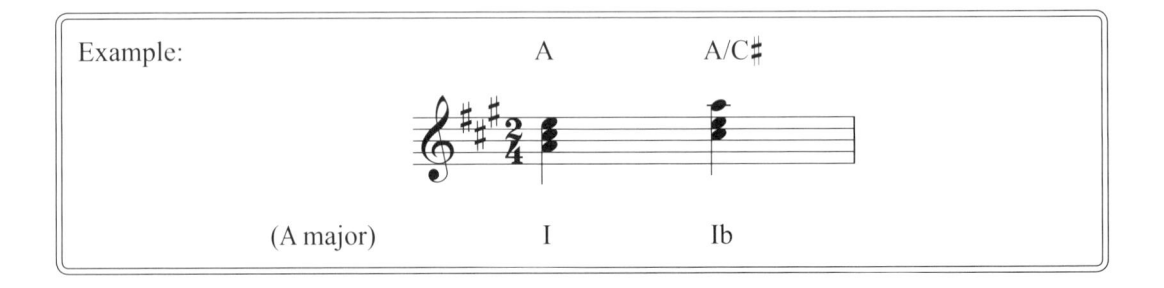

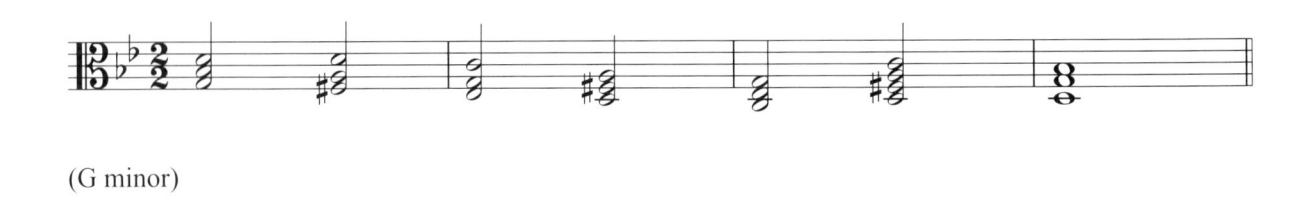

Example:

        A   A/C♯

(A major)   I   Ib

(G minor)

4. Name the key and cadence.

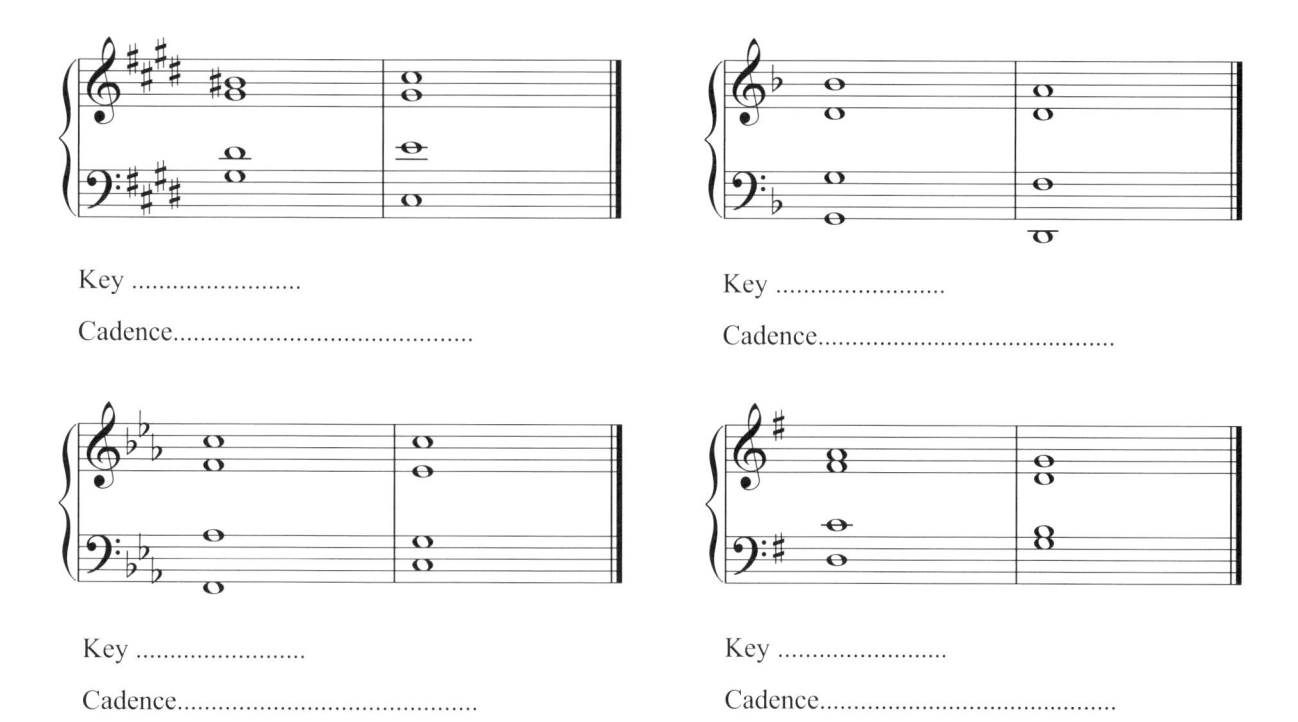

Key ....

Cadence..

Key ....

Cadence..

Key ....

Cadence..

Key ....

Cadence..

5 a) Use the root of each chord shown by the Roman numerals to write a bass line.

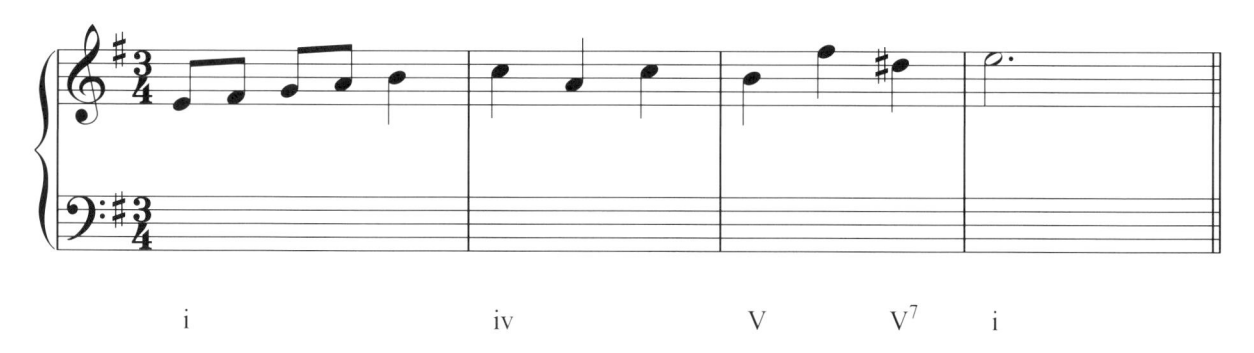

        i   iv   V   V^7 i

b) Use notes from the chords shown by the chord symbols to write a tune above the bass line. Add some unaccented passing notes.

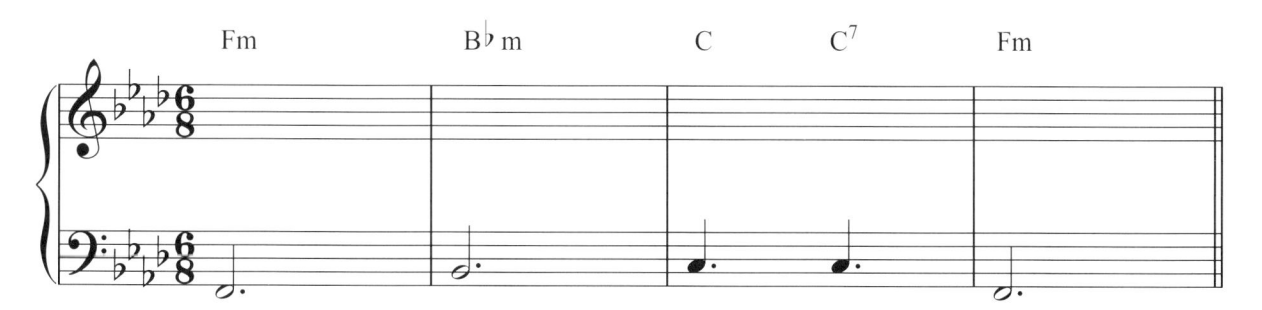

Fm   B♭m   C   C^7 Fm

6 a) Transpose the following melody up a perfect 5th so that a French horn player will be able to play it at the same pitch as the following notes.

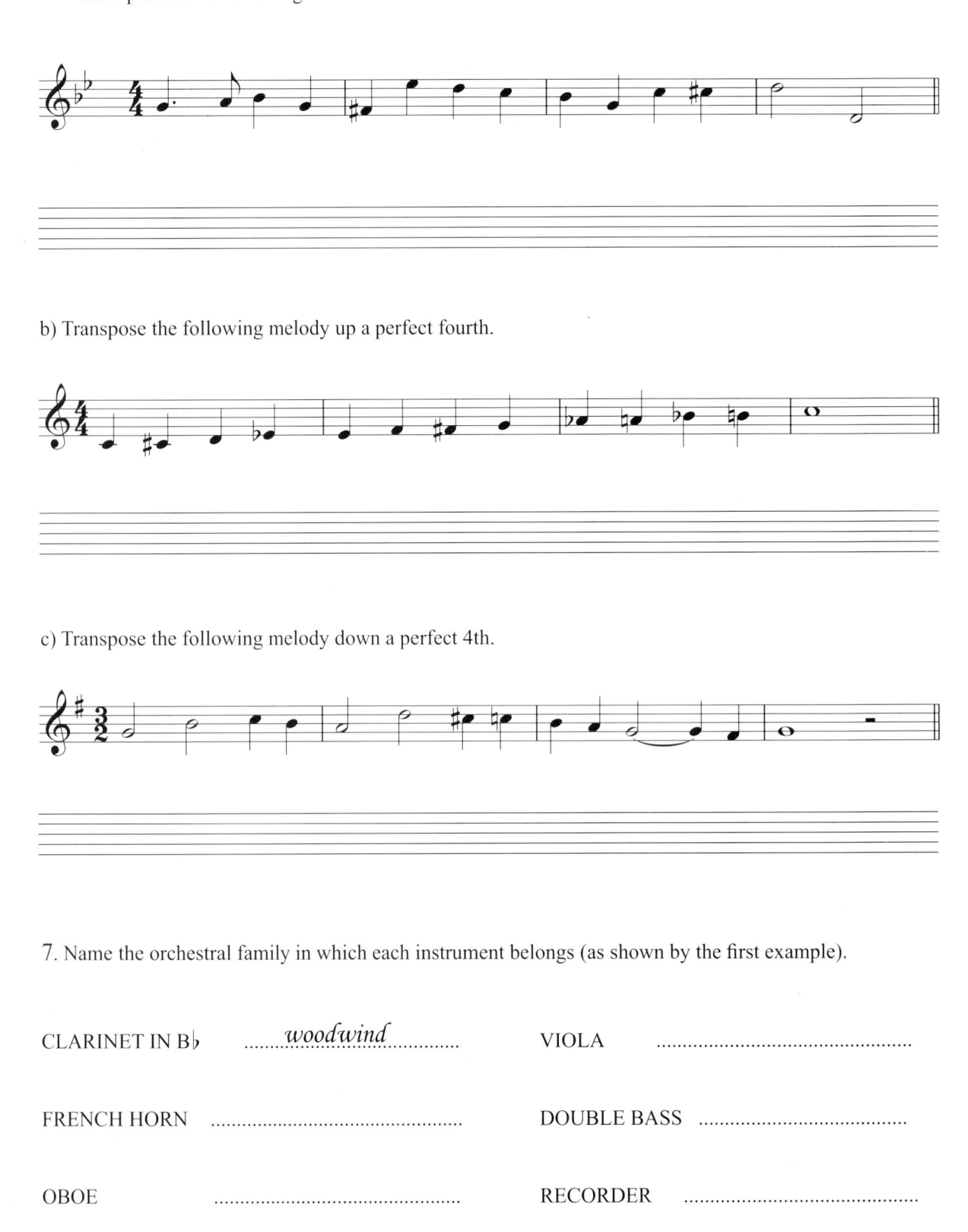

b) Transpose the following melody up a perfect fourth.

c) Transpose the following melody down a perfect 4th.

7. Name the orchestral family in which each instrument belongs (as shown by the first example).

CLARINET IN B♭	*woodwind*	VIOLA	....
FRENCH HORN	....	DOUBLE BASS	....
OBOE	....	RECORDER	....